Hebrew
Manuscript Painting

DAVID GOLDSTEIN

The British Library

© 1985 The British Library Board

Published by
The British Library
Reference Division Publications
Great Russell Street
London WC1B 3DG

and 51 Washington Street
Dover, New Hampshire 03820

British Library Cataloguing in
Publication Data

Goldstein, David, *1933*.
  Hebrew manuscript painting.
  I. Illumination of books and manuscripts: Jewish
  I. Title
  745.6′7′09174924   ND2935.

  ISBN 0-7123-0054-6.

Library of Congress Cataloging in
Publication Data

Goldstein, David, *1933*–
  Hebrew Manuscript Painting.

  Bibliography: P.
  1. Illumination of books and
manuscripts, Hebrew. I. Title.
ND2935.G65   1985   745.6′74924
  85-18995
ISBN 0-7123-0054-6 (Pbk.)

Designed by Roger Davies
Typeset in Monophoto Ehrhardt by August
Filmsetting, Haydock,
St. Helens
Origination by York House Graphics, Hanwell
Printed and bound in Great Britain by William
Clowes Ltd., Beccles

Contents

בְּתֵּינוּ הִצִּיל וַיִּקֹּד הָעָם וַיִּשְׁתַּחֲווּ

מצה זו

שֶׁאָנוּ

אוֹכְלִין

מַהֵנ

שֶׁלֹּא

עַל שׁוּם

שׁוּם

הִסְפִּיק

בְּצֵקָם

Introduction

Art has been an important element in Jewish creativity from the earliest times. The Hebrew Bible itself is a witness. It tells us of the strange creatures called 'cherubim' whose outstretched wings sheltered the ark of the covenant from above. The candelabrum in the sanctuary is described with meticulous detail and was clearly an object on which great artistic ingenuity and care were expended. The construction of the tabernacle and its furniture was entrusted to Bezalel ben Uri, a man who was pre-eminent 'in wisdom, understanding, and knowledge, and in all manner of workmanship; able to design skilful work, in gold, silver and brass, to cut precious stones, and to carve wood'.

Jewish art in the ancient world

Solomon's Temple in Jerusalem, so lavishly described in the Bible, had a great laver which rested on the backs of twelve oxen. The temple must have been one of the architectural and artistic wonders of the ancient world. Only descriptions are left to convey to us the fruits of early Hebrew artistic endeavour, since very little has physically survived destruction by enemies and the depredations of the ages.

But we can still see the remains of synagogues constructed in early post-Biblical times which show a highly developed artistic sense. Most remarkable are the series of wall-paintings in the synagogue of Dura-Europos on the Euphrates, which depict Biblical narratives often enhanced by elements drawn from rabbinic interpretations and embellishment. These date from the 3rd century AD and they may reflect earlier traditions. Mosaic floors in the synagogues at Naarah in the Jordan valley (5th century), at Beth-Shean (5th century) and Beth-Alfa (6th century) both in the Valley of Jezreel, also display representations of Biblical scenes as well as of the Temple and its furniture, and signs of the Zodiac. We are safe in assuming, therefore, that in these centuries the artistic adornment of places of worship was a feature of Jewish life, and the fact that there are few references to these specific features in contemporary Jewish literature, either in praise or blame, lead us to conclude that they were an accepted part of normal daily living.

1 Golden Haggadah.
A representation of 'this *matsah* (unleavened bread)'.
North Spain, Barcelona (?);
about 1320.
[Add. MS 27210, f.44v.]

East and West

We can, however, trace no direct connection between the art of this period and that of the illuminated Hebrew manuscripts which are the subject of this book. This is due to two separate but complementary factors. The first is that the Jews of the Near East came swiftly under the influence of Islam from the 7th century onwards. Islam's very strict prohibition of figurative art had a profound influence on the Jews under its sway, and, as we shall see, this influence exerted itself for many centuries. The second factor was the unease felt by the rabbis at the apparent transgression by the artist of the second commandment: 'You shall not make for yourself a sculptured image, or any likeness of anything that is in heaven above, or in the earth beneath, or in the water under the earth'.

This commandment is, of course, at the root of Islamic susceptibilities, but the rabbis had a more difficult task because they were religious leaders of Jewish communities who in the early middle ages spread far and wide throughout the continent of Europe, and who thus came into contact with Christian societies which had developed a flourishing artistic culture.

Many and varied were the questions addressed to rabbis on the topic of Jewish representational art, and many and varied were the replies. Generally speaking, the rabbinic response was to forbid out of hand three-dimensional artistic forms since these clearly contravened the biblical prohibition of 'sculptured' images. In Western Europe (but not in Islamic countries) representational painting was tolerated grudgingly, provided that the 'images' so formed were not intended to be objects of worship, or likely to distract the Jew from concentrating on the true purpose of his devotions. There was always room for local divergencies in rabbinic pronouncements, and there is no doubt that the ensuing controversies delayed the appearance of a Jewish tradition of manuscript painting in the West. Indeed, there are Jewish communities to this day who are firmly opposed to representational art.

It is to Western Europe that we must look for the finest examples of Hebrew manuscript painting, but the earliest manifestations of the art appear in the Middle East. Fragments of Biblical manuscripts of the 10th and 11th centuries from Egypt show typical Islamic-style decorations, with highly ornamented 'carpet-pages'. This tradition of decoration persisted for several centuries among Jewish communities who lived in an Islamic environment and is particularly noticeable in the Yemen (3) where Jews copied their sacred scriptures by hand down to modern times. The depiction of the Temple implements is also known in an early Egyptian Hebrew Bible fragment now in Leningrad, and the tradition found its way later to Spain (19, 20). Only in Persia among Islamic countries do we find a Jewish figurative tradition (32).

When we turn to the Western world we see that here too the decoration and illustration of Hebrew manuscripts were profoundly influenced by the methods and styles of the host cultures. There is little that is unique and distinctive in Hebrew manuscript art, except for the use of micrographic designs and figurations (9, 10, 22). Special characteristics are to be found in the content and subject-matter to which the art is applied, rather than in the techniques and styles employed.

Hebrew script

The most obvious distinctive feature is the Hebrew alphabet itself. Abundant love and care were lavished on the script – which has a certain sanctity, since Hebrew is a 'holy tongue'. The forms of the letters lend themselves to decoration and embellishment. The round or square letters can carry within them flowers or stars or even representations of religious ritual (44, 45). The long down strokes of the letter *kuf* and of some of the final letters are continued into leafy tendrils, or are used to form fanciful birds and other animals, or human grotesques. The same is true of the upstroke of the letter *lamed*. Occasionally a scribe will use letters in a zoomorphic form for his colophon.

Capital letters are not used in Hebrew script, and therefore Jewish scribes unlike their Christian counterparts did not usually enlarge the initials of a particular book or chapter. They emphasised instead the whole initial word (for example, 5 and 6). Where a decorated initial letter is found this can be put down to Christian influence.

Making the manuscript

In the making of an illuminated Hebrew manuscript the most important part was played by the scribe (*sofer*), not the artist. However aesthetically pleasing the illuminations may be and however striking the illustrations, we must not lose sight of the fact that it is the text that is the basic and indeed most valuable element. Only perhaps in the micrographic designs of the *masorah* (see below) did art predominate over text.

The scribe therefore was master of the manuscript. He not only wrote the text but planned the whole layout, leaving spaces for illustrations and sometimes writing captions for the artist by way of instruction as to the subject he wished to see represented. Often the scribe restricted himself to writing the consonantal text; the vowels and other markings, which are written below, inside or above the consonants, being added later by a 'pointer' or 'punctuator' (*nakdan*). This second hand might also copy a commentary in the margins of the manuscript and, in the case of Biblical texts, add the *masorah*. Jewish scribes worked individually, the tradition being passed from father to son, and there is no record of *scriptoria* (writing workshops) on the Christian model.

Sometimes the scribe and artist were one and the same, but this is not usual. In most cases the identity of the artist is unknown, his work not being thought sufficiently important to warrant attribution. The artists were not always Jews. Non-Jews were frequently employed by patrons to decorate manuscripts, and it is not surprising therefore to find clear examples of Christian iconography, particularly in illustrations of Biblical scenes. Frequently too a manuscript was worked by more than one artist. If the artists were Christians, a school with a master and assistants might be involved. Alternatively, additional work might be done as the manuscript travelled from place to place or from hand to hand. This was a frequent occurrence, because of the often enforced peregrinations of Jewish communities. A Bible, now in the Bibliothèque Nationale in Paris (Cod. Heb. 15) began life in Lisbon, but, the Jews being expelled from Portugal in 1497, it received most of its decoration in Italy. Similarly an artist might himself travel from one area to another and be influenced by local styles of painting. Such a painter was Joel ben Simeon Feibusch, who journeyed more than once to Northern Italy from his home in the Rhineland, and his work shows evidence of this. Some of his manuscripts were additionally worked by other hands at a later date (**front cover**).

We can, however distinguish some major centres of Hebrew manuscript painting which display a good measure of internal consistency.

Sefardim and Ashkenazim

In Jewish history generally two streams of religious and communal endeavour are apparent: the Sefardi and Ashkenazi. The first originated in the Jewish communities of the Babylonian diaspora and came to be associated specifically with the Mediterranean world, particularly the Iberian peninsula and North Africa. The Ashkenazi had its roots in Palestinian Judaism, and the bearers of this tradition in the diaspora travelled from Italy to the Rhineland, so that the term is now applied generally to the Jews of North and East Europe, and in our context particularly to those of Germany and Northern France.

Although the beliefs and religious practices of the Sefardim and the Ashkenazim are basically identical, both going back to the sacred writings of the Bible, Talmud, and legal codes, there are minor differences between them in liturgical rites and other customs, and these differences have a bearing on their manuscript traditions.

In general the Sefardi scribes used reed pens, while the Ashkenazim used quills.

This meant that the letters of the former were of equal thickness throughout, while the latter were able to taper theirs, particularly in their downstrokes. Ashkenazi script in this and other ways shows a similarity to medieval Latin uncial script. These factors influenced the way in which the letters were embellished by the artist.

2 Coburg Pentateuch. Teacher and pupil. There is a touch of humour in the illustration, since the pupil is studying Hillel's Golden Rule: 'What is hateful to you, do not do to another'. The building in the background is probably the Veste Coburg (Coburg Castle). Copied by Simhah ben Samuel Halevi. Coburg; dated 1395. [Add. MS 19776, f.72v.]

וּבַהֲמִיּה וּבְשָׂדְּהוּ אֲחֻזָּתוֹ לֹא יִמָּכֵר וְלֹא יִגָּאֵל כָּל חֵרֶם קֹדֶשׁ קָדָשִׁים הוּא לַיהוָה כָּל חֵרֶם אֲשֶׁר

יׇחֳרַם מִן הָאָדָם לֹא יִפָּדֶה מוֹת יוּמָת וְכׇל מַעְשַׂר הָאָרֶץ מִזֶּרַע הָאָרֶץ מִפְּרִי הָעֵץ לַיהוָה

הוּא קֹדֶשׁ לַיהוָה וְאִם גָּאֹל יִגְאַל אִישׁ מִמַּעַשְׂרוֹ חֲמִישִׁתוֹ יֹסֵף עָלָיו וְכׇל מַעְשַׂר בָּקָר

וָצֹאן כֹּל אֲשֶׁר יַעֲבֹר תַּחַת הַשָּׁבֶט הָעֲשִׂירִי יִהְיֶה קֹּדֶשׁ לַיהוָה לֹא יְבַקֵּר בֵּין טוֹב לָרַע וְלֹא

יְמִירֶנּוּ וְאִם הָמֵר יְמִירֶנּוּ וְהָיָה הוּא וּתְמוּרָתוֹ יִהְיֶה קֹדֶשׁ לֹא יִגָּאֵל אֵלֶּה הַמִּצְוֹת אֲשֶׁר

צִוָּה יְהוָה אֶת מֹשֶׁה אֶל בְּנֵי יִשְׂרָאֵל בְּהַר סִינָי

חזק

סִימָן סְכוּם פְּסוּקֵי דְסִפְרָא גֹטָ"ר

3 San'a Pentateuch.
Part of a carpet-page with
Arabic text giving details of
the colophon. Copied
apparently by Benayah ben
Se'adyah. San'a in the
Yemen; dated 1469.
[Or. MS 2348, f.154v.]

The Sefardi style of manuscript illumination, emanating principally from Spain and Portugal, displays the influence of Muslim art. Although most of the extant Hebrew illuminated manuscripts from this region originated after the Reconquest, when the Arabs had been driven out of the peninsula, the influence of their culture remained. We find many pages with arabesques, filigree work and geometrical patterns (**26, 27, 55, 56**) that can be paralleled in manuscripts of the Koran and other Arabic works. Manuscript pages are framed in borders that are clearly inspired by Muslim architecture.

The manuscripts illuminated in Lisbon come from the last decades of Jewish life there (before their expulsion in 1497) and give evidence of a prosperous, settled culture. Some of the motifs used also appear in early Hebrew printing in the peninsula.

Figurative art, particularly in the Spanish *haggadot*, shows other influences. The posture and grouping as well as the painting style of many of the figures in the Golden Haggadah, for example, are similar to those of French Gothic (**46**), while Byzantine influence can be seen in the pictures in the Catalan Haggadah (**42**).

The Gothic style can be seen also in Ashkenazi Hebrew manuscripts, most noticeably in the North French Miscellany (for example, **16, 17, 18**), which has very strong parallels with Christian religous art of the late 13th century from this region.

The artistic elements in Italian Hebrew manuscripts are not easy to ascribe to either the Ashkenazi or the Sefardi traditions. Jews from both areas, often fleeing persecution, joined their brethren who had been settled in Italy since Roman times, and therefore we find both kinds of religious rite flourishing there, in addition to an indigenous Jewish Italian one. The artistic features of these manuscripts bear the unmistakeable impress of Renaissance Italian styles, particularly in their borders of delicately painted flowers and animals (53). Indeed many of the Hebrew manuscripts from Italy were undoubtedly painted by non-Jews.

In our discussion of Hebrew illuminated manuscripts in the British Library we shall cut across geographical and communal differentiations and examine instead the types of text that were illuminated, namely, Bibles, prayer-books, and some other miscellaneous items.

Bibles

Particular love and care were lavished on the copying of manuscripts of the Bible, the most sacred possession of the Jewish people. The Bible comprises, according to Jewish tradition, 24 books in three major sections: the Pentateuch (*Torah*); Former and Latter Prophets; and Hagiographa (or writings). The last includes five books, namely, Song of Songs, Ruth, Lamentations, Ecclesiastes and Esther, which are called specifically *megillot* (scrolls). One of these is read at five different dates in the Jewish year, and they are therefore frequently included in prayerbooks containing liturgies for those occasions.

Specific sanctity attaches to the *Torah*, sometimes known as the Five Books of Moses, for the traditional Jewish view is that Moses wrote them at divine dictation. The *Torah* is divided into weekly portions, and is read in the synagogues. For this purpose it is still written on vellum by hand in scroll form, and called the *Sefer Torah* (Book of the *Torah*). (The Book of Esther is also written for synagogal use in the form of a scroll). The reading from the Torah is followed by a passage (called *haftarah*) from the prophetical books.

Manuscripts of the Hebrew Bible can therefore be of several kinds: a *Sefer Torah* in scroll form, which is never illuminated; a complete Bible in 24 books; the Pentateuch on its own, or together with prophetical readings for the various Sabbaths, and the five *megillot*; the Prophets and the Hagiographa on their own; or other combinations of one or more individual books.

Since it is a religious duty to read the weekly portion of the Torah in Aramaic translation (*Targum*), this is sometimes included in the manuscript. The text might also be accompanied by a rabbinic commentary.

For a scribe, the writing of the Bible is a task which demands the utmost concentration and attention to detail. Minute observation was therefore applied in order to ensure that the text was copied and read correctly. This work of examination and annotation was

4, 5 Duke of Sussex
German Pentateuch.
Right: decorated first
word of the Book of
Leviticus. *Opposite*:
Decorated first word of
the Book of Exodus.
Copied and probably
illuminated by Hayyim.
South Germany; about
1300.
[Add. MS 15282, ff.137r, 75v.]

accomplished by the masoretes who lived in Babylonia and Palestine from the 6th to the 9th centuries AD. The record of their achievement is preserved in the notes called the *masorah*, which surrounds the Biblical text and contains guidance as to the writing of specific words and their pronunciation, notes on the frequency of rarer words, remarks on different scribal traditions and so on. It is to the masoretes too that we owe the 'pointing' of the text, that is, the supply of vowels and other marks which aid pronunciation and grammatical accuracy.

It is the *masorah* which is frequently used in Hebrew manuscripts for micrographic designs. Other scribal traditions also use writing in order to form pictures, but their method usually is to adjust the length of lines in order to create an object which can then, if required, be indicated additionally in outline. Jewish scribes did this too, but their unique contribution was to make designs by writing continuously in tiny script, often weaving the most intricate patterns. This can be seen very well in German Bibles, where we find pictures in micrography of a falconer on horseback, a knight jousting, Jonah and the whale (10), or architectural motifs (22). Sefardi Bibles had a long tradition of micrographic design, going back at least to Egypt in the 11th century. The San'a Pentateuch uses the text of Psalms for this purpose (12), and the Lisbon Bible a poem (27); and the *masorah* is often similarly utilised by Jewish scribes in Spain.

Illustrations of Biblical narratives are uncommon in Sefardi Bibles, and are also quite rare in Ashkenazi ones. They are far more common in *Haggadot*, and we shall describe these below. In Bibles we see some of the tribes with their standards depicted in the Duke of Sussex German Pentateuch (8), whereas in the Coburg Pentateuch the empty spaces at the end of each book are used for illustrations that have little or no relevance to the Pentateuch at all (2, 11).

An exception should be made of the North French Miscellany. Although this manuscript is not strictly Biblical in the sense that the others are, because it contains much else besides, nonetheless its illustrations are abundant and include many that are scriptural (13–18). This remarkable manuscript measures only 160 × 120 mm; yet it contains 749 leaves of the most delicate vellum. The greater part was written by a scribe named Benjamin. There are 41 full-page illuminations as well as a large number of marginal decorations. The paintings were executed by more than one artist, and most of them are attributable to the last 20 years of the 13th century. The strong influence of contemporary Christian styles is undoubted, but it remains unclear whether the artists themselves were Christians or Jews.

6 Duke of Sussex German Pentateuch.
Beginning of the Book of Ecclesiastes, one of the *megillot* (scrolls) at the end of the manuscript. The figure resembles contemporary representations of King David, but is meant to portray King Solomon, to whom Ecclesiastes is traditionally ascribed.
[Add. MS 15282, f.302r. Detail.]

7 (*Overleaf left*): Duke of Sussex German Pentateuch.
Decorated first word of the Book of Deuteronomy.
[Add. MS 15282 f.238 recto.]

8 (*Overleaf right*): Duke of Sussex German Pentateuch.
Decorated first word of the Book of Numbers. The knights represent the tribes of Israel with their banners.
[Add. MS 15282, f.179v.]

A striking feature of Hebrew Bibles from Spain is the opening double-page spread of the vessels of the Temple (**19, 20**). These Bibles are of great size and weight, and must surely have been intended for use on a Synagogue lectern. The Temple's appurtenances are sometimes depicted in gold leaf on a tessellated background, and they include many of the items described in scriptural passages concerning the Tabernacle in the wilderness as well as Solomon's Temple, and the second Temple too, whose details are described in rabbinic texts. Painting such as this may have messianic significance, for the rebuilding of the Temple is an integral part of the traditional Jewish messianic expectation. This kind of Bible is called, in fact, 'The Temple of the Lord'.

By far the greater part of the illumination in Hebrew Bible manuscripts is restricted to the decoration of the opening words of each book (for example, **4, 5**). Italian Bibles are often superbly embellished in this way, the artists using delicate floral and animal motifs. Sometimes the Song of Moses at the Red Sea (Exodus, chapter 15) is singled out for special attention. The Lisbon Bibles, dating from the second half of the 15th century, are also very heavily decorated with foliage, flowers, and birds and intricate arabesques and filigree work. Often the artist leaves the opening of the Book of Lamentations quite plain because the nature of the text hardly calls for beautification, and also because it is read on the ninth of the month Av, a day of fasting in commemmoration of the destruction of the Temple in Jerusalem (but see **26**). On the other

17

9 Former and Latter
Prophets, and
Hagiographa.
Beginning of the Book of Ruth,
with designs in micrography,
using the textual notes and
comments known as the *masorah*.
Ashkenazi (Franco–German)
hand. 13th Century.
[Or. MS 2091, f.268r. (Detail).]

10 Pentateuch with
prophetical readings and
the Five Scrolls.
Book of Jonah, Chapters 1 and 2.
Jonah and the whale. A drawing
in micrography using the textual
notes and comments known as
the *masorah*. Written in an
Ashkenazi (Franco–German)
hand; 13th–14th century.
[Add. MS 21160, f.292r. Detail.]

11 Coburg Pentateuch.
A representation apparently of
King Solomon on his throne.
According to Jewish legend there
were animals on the steps who
raised Solomon to the throne.
Copied by Simhah ben Samuel
Halevi. Coburg; dated 1395.
[Add. MS 19776, f.54v. Detail.]

12 San'a Pentateuch.
Frontispiece with micrographic
designs representing fish and
mountains (or fish-scales?). The
texts are drawn principally from
Psalms 119, 121 and 122. Copied
apparently by Benayah ben
Se'adyah. San'a in the Yemen;
dated 1469.
[Or. MS 2348, f.39r.]

רב קטן

זה עץ כתוך הזיבה · והיונה עליו נחה ·

13 North French Miscellany.
Noah's Ark.
The raven perches on the roof and the dove
returns with an olive-leaf. The waters have
receded. North France; about 1280.
[Add. MS 11639, f.521r.]

14 North French Miscellany.
David and Goliath.
The caption reads 'This is Goliath the Philistine,
and David aiming at him, surrounded by his dog
and rams'. North France; about 1280.
[Add. MS 11639, f.523v.]

זה גלית הפלשתי ודוד הזורק לו
וכלב והאיל סביבו

15 North French Miscellany.
King David and his harp.
North France; about 1280.
[Add. MS 11639, f.117v.]

זה דוד המנגן בנבל ׃

זה "האיש וחוה ערומים ועץ הדעת והנחש"

זה שמשון הרוכב על הארי ויקרע לידו

16, 17, 18 North French Miscellany.

Left: Adam, Eve and the serpent with the Tree of Knowledge. The serpent, before the divine curse, had legs, and is thus depicted here (Enlarged). *Right, above*: Samson and the lion. *Right, below*: King Solomon judging between the two women.
[Add. MS 11639, ff. 520v, 520r, 518r.]

זה שלמה המלך העושה משפט משתי נשים

19, 20 (*Overleaf*): Duke of Sussex Spanish Bible.

Left: the vessels of the Temple. *Right*: the candelabrum (*Menorah*) and other vessels of the Temple. Catalonia; mid-14th century.
[Add. MS 15250, ff.4r, 3v.]

24

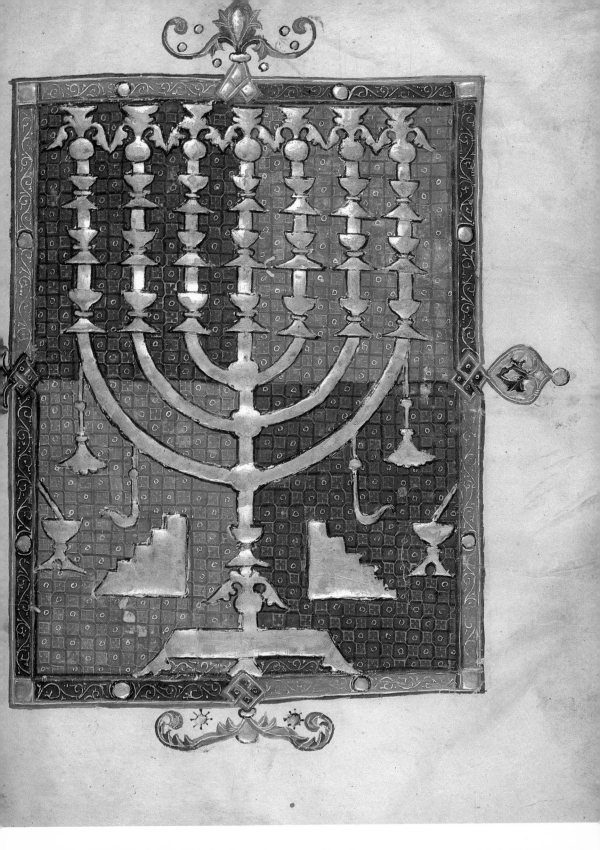

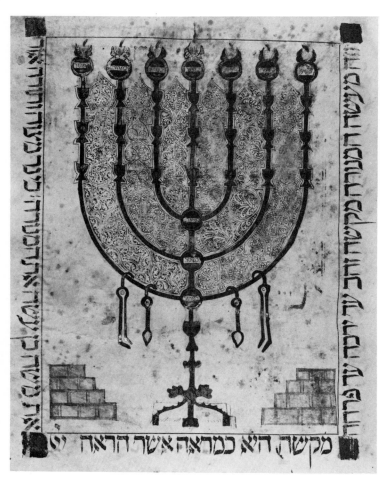

21 Bible.
The Temple candelabrum
(*Menorah*). Copied by Jacob
ben Joseph of Ripoll for Isaac
ben Judah of Tolosa
(Toulouse?). Solsona, Spain;
dated 1384.
[Kings MS 1, f.3r.]

**22 Pentateuch with
prophetical readings and
the Five Scrolls.**
End of the Book of Ruth. An
elaborate design in
micrography using the textual
notes and comments known
as the *masorah*. Written in an
Ashkenazi (Franco–German)
hand; 13th–14th century.
[Add. MS 21160, f.300v.]

וַיִּ֨קַּ֧ח יְהֹוָ֛ה לָ֖הּ הֵרָי֑וֹן וַתֵּ֥לֶ
בֵ֖ן ׀ וַתֹּאמַ֣רְנָה הַנָּשִׁ֗ים
לְנׇעֳמִ֞י בָּר֣וּךְ יְהֹוָה֮ אֲשֶׁ֣ר
לֹ֣א הִשְׁבִּ֣ית לָךְ֮ גֹּאֵל֒ הַיּ֖וֹם
וְשִׂרֵ֥א שְׁמ֖וֹ בְּיִשְׂרָאֵ֑ל
וְהָ֤יָה לָךְ֙ לְמֵשִׁ֣יב נֶ֔פֶשׁ
וּלְכַלְכֵּ֖ל אֶת־שֵׂיבָתֵ֑ךְ כִּ֣י כַלָּתֵ֤ךְ אֲשֶֽׁר
אֲשֶׁ֣ר אֲהֵבַ֔תֶךְ יְלָדַ֔תּוּ
אֲ֠שֶׁ֠ר הִ֣יא ט֤וֹבָה לָ֔ךְ
מִשִּׁבְעָ֖ה בָּנִֽים וַתִּקַּ֨ח
נׇעֳמִ֤י אֶת־הַיֶּ֙לֶד֙ וַתְּשִׁתֵ֣הוּ
בְחֵיקָ֔הּ וַתְּהִי־ל֖וֹ לְאֹמַֽנֶת
וַתִּקְרֶ֩אנָה֩ ל֨וֹ הַשְּׁכֵנ֥וֹת
שֵׁם֙ לֵאמֹ֔ר יֻלַּד־בֵּ֖ן לְנׇעֳמִ֑י
וַתִּקְרֶ֤אנָֽה שְׁמוֹ֙ עוֹבֵ֔ד
ה֥וּא אֲבִי־יִשַׁ֖י אֲבִ֥י דָוִֽד ׀
וְאֵ֙לֶּה֙
תּוֹלְד֣וֹת פָּ֔רֶץ פֶּ֖רֶץ הוֹלִ֥י
ד אֶת־חֶצְר֑וֹן וְחֶצְר֖וֹ
הוֹלִ֥יד אֶת־רָ֔ם וְרָ֖ם הוֹלִ֥יד
אֶת־עַמִּֽינָדָֽב ׀ וְעַמִּֽינָדָב֙
הוֹלִ֥יד אֶת־נַחְשׁ֔וֹן וְנַחְשׁ֖וֹן
הוֹלִ֥יד אֶת־שַׂלְמָ֑ה וְשַׂלְמוֹ֙
הוֹלִ֥יד אֶת־בֹּ֔עַז וּבֹ֖עַז הוֹלִ֥
הוֹלִ֥יד אֶת־עוֹבֵ֑ד וְעֹבֵ֖
הוֹלִ֥יד אֶת־יִשָׁ֑י וְיִשַׁ֖י כד
הוֹלִ֥יד אֶת־דָּוִֽד ׀

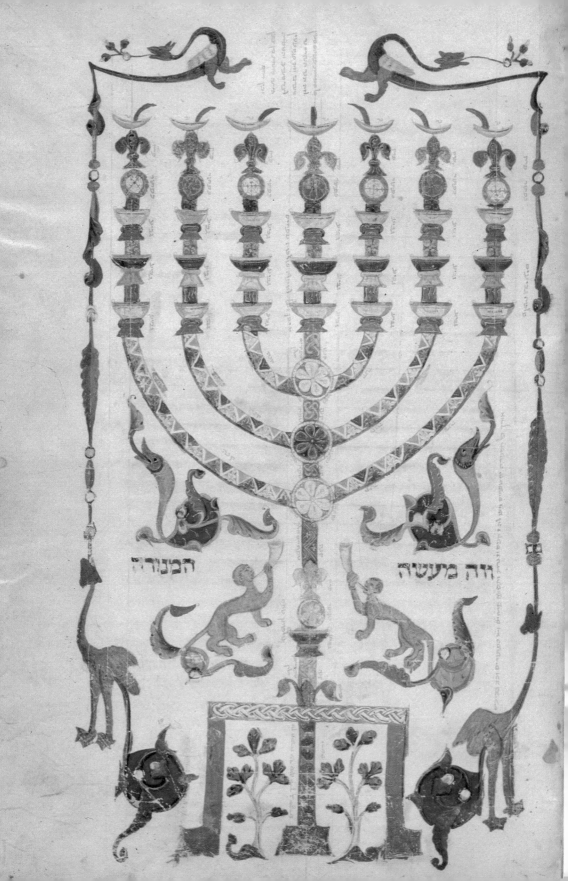

23 (*Left*): Bible. In two
volumes.
The Temple candelabrum
(*Menorah*). The tripod
supporting it is a distinctive
feature (compare **21** and **20**).
Italy; about 1300.
[Harley MS 5710 (Vol. 1), f.136r.]

24 (*Right*): Bible. In two
volumes.
Opening of the Book of
Proverbs. Italy; about 1300.
[Harley MS 5711 (Vol 2), f.241v.]

25 (*Overleaf, left*):
Lisbon Bible
3 volumes.
Beginning of the Book of
Joshua. Copied by Samuel
Ibn Musa for Joseph al-
Hakim. Lisbon; completed in
1482.
[Or. 2627 (Vol. 2), f.1v.]

26 (*Overleaf, right*):
Pentateuch, with
prophetical readings
and the Five Scrolls.
Beginning of the Book of
Lamentations. Spain;
14th–15th century.
[Add. MS 27167, f.419v.]

איכה ישבה בדד העיר

רבתי עם היתה כאלמנה רבתי בגוים
שרתי במדינות היתה למס
בכה תבכה בלילה ודמעתה על

27 (*Above*): Lisbon Bible. 3 Volumes.
An imaginary debate between the Bible and the Talmud, written in elaborate micrographic form. Copied by Samuel Ibn Musa for Joseph al-Hakim. Lisbon; completed in 1482.
[Or. 2628 (Vol 3), f.185r.]

28 (*Right*): Duke of Sussex Italian Bible.
Beginning of Book of Genesis. Copied by Moses Akrish. Italy; dated 1448.
[Add. MS 15251, f.13r.]

בָּרָא אֱלֹהִים אֵת הַשָּׁמַיִם וְאֵת הָאָרֶץ
וְהָאָרֶץ הָיְתָה תֹהוּ וָבֹהוּ וְחֹשֶׁךְ עַל
פְּנֵי תְהוֹם וְרוּחַ אֱלֹהִים מְרַחֶפֶת עַל
פְּנֵי הַמָּיִם וַיֹּאמֶר אֱלֹהִים יְהִי אוֹר
וַיְהִי אוֹר וַיַּרְא אֱלֹהִים אֶת הָאוֹר
כִּי טוֹב וַיַּבְדֵּל אֱלֹהִים בֵּין הָאוֹר
וּבֵין הַחֹשֶׁךְ וַיִּקְרָא אֱלֹהִים לָאוֹר
יוֹם וְלַחֹשֶׁךְ קָרָא לָיְלָה וַיְהִי עֶרֶב
וַיְהִי בֹקֶר יוֹם אֶחָד
וַיֹּאמֶר אֱלֹהִים יְהִי רָקִיעַ בְּתוֹךְ הַמָּיִם
וִיהִי מַבְדִּיל בֵּין מַיִם לָמָיִם וַיַּעַשׂ
אֱלֹהִים אֶת הָרָקִיעַ וַיַּבְדֵּל בֵּין הַמַּיִם
אֲשֶׁר מִתַּחַת לָרָקִיעַ וּבֵין הַמַּיִם אֲשֶׁר
מֵעַל לָרָקִיעַ וַיְהִי כֵן וַיִּקְרָא אֱלֹהִים
לָרָקִיעַ שָׁמָיִם וַיְהִי עֶרֶב וַיְהִי בֹקֶר
יוֹם שֵׁנִי
וַיֹּאמֶר אֱלֹהִים יִקָּווּ הַמַּיִם מִתַּחַת
הַשָּׁמַיִם אֶל מָקוֹם אֶחָד וְתֵרָאֶה
הַיַּבָּשָׁה וַיְהִי כֵן וַיִּקְרָא אֱלֹהִים
לַיַּבָּשָׁה אֶרֶץ וּלְמִקְוֵה הַמַּיִם קָרָא
יַמִּים וַיַּרְא אֱלֹהִים כִּי טוֹב וַיֹּאמֶר

אֱלֹהִים תַּדְשֵׁא הָאָרֶץ דֶּשֶׁא עֵשֶׂב
מַזְרִיעַ זֶרַע עֵץ פְּרִי עֹשֶׂה פְּרִי לְמִינוֹ
אֲשֶׁר זַרְעוֹ בוֹ עַל הָאָרֶץ וַיְהִי כֵן
וַתּוֹצֵא הָאָרֶץ דֶּשֶׁא עֵשֶׂב מַזְרִיעַ זֶרַע
לְמִינֵהוּ וְעֵץ עֹשֶׂה פְּרִי אֲשֶׁר זַרְעוֹ בוֹ
לְמִינֵהוּ וַיַּרְא אֱלֹהִים כִּי טוֹב וַיְהִי
עֶרֶב וַיְהִי בֹקֶר יוֹם שְׁלִישִׁי
וַיֹּאמֶר אֱלֹהִים יְהִי מְאֹרֹת בִּרְקִיעַ
הַשָּׁמַיִם לְהַבְדִּיל בֵּין הַיּוֹם וּבֵין הַלָּיְלָה
וְהָיוּ לְאֹתֹת וּלְמוֹעֲדִים וּלְיָמִים וְשָׁנִים
וְהָיוּ לִמְאוֹרֹת בִּרְקִיעַ הַשָּׁמַיִם
לְהָאִיר עַל הָאָרֶץ וַיְהִי כֵן וַיַּעַשׂ
אֱלֹהִים אֶת שְׁנֵי הַמְּאֹרֹת הַגְּדֹלִים
אֶת הַמָּאוֹר הַגָּדֹל לְמֶמְשֶׁלֶת הַיּוֹם
וְאֶת הַמָּאוֹר הַקָּטֹן לְמֶמְשֶׁלֶת
הַלָּיְלָה וְאֵת הַכּוֹכָבִים וַיִּתֵּן אֹתָם
אֱלֹהִים בִּרְקִיעַ הַשָּׁמָיִם לְהָאִיר עַל
הָאָרֶץ וְלִמְשֹׁל בַּיּוֹם וּבַלַּיְלָה
וּלְהַבְדִּיל בֵּין הָאוֹר וּבֵין הַחֹשֶׁךְ וַיַּרְא
אֱלֹהִים כִּי טוֹב וַיְהִי עֶרֶב וַיְהִי בֹקֶר
יוֹם רְבִיעִי

יְעֹרְרוּ וְיַֽעֲלוּ הַגּוֹיִם אֶל עֵמֶק יְהוֹשָׁפָט כִּי שָׁם אֵשֵׁב
לִשְׁפֹּט אֶת כָּל הַגּוֹיִם מִסָּבִיב ׀ שִׁלְחוּ מַגָּל כִּי בָשַׁל
קָצִיר בֹּאוּ רְדוּ כִּי מָלְאָה גַּת הֵשִׁיקוּ הַיְקָבִים כִּי רַבָּה
רָעָתָם ׀ הֲמוֹנִים הֲמוֹנִים בְּעֵמֶק הֶחָרוּץ כִּי קָרוֹב יוֹם
יְהוֹה בְּעֵמֶק הֶחָרוּץ ׀ שֶׁמֶשׁ וְיָרֵחַ קָדָרוּ וְכוֹכָבִים
אָסְפוּ נָגְהָם ׀ וַיהוֹה מִצִּיּוֹן יִשְׁאָג וּמִירוּשָׁלִַם יִתֵּן
קוֹלוֹ וְרָעֲשׁוּ שָׁמַיִם וָאָרֶץ וַיהוֹה מַחֲסֶה לְעַמּוֹ ׀
וּמָעוֹז לִבְנֵי יִשְׂרָאֵל ׀ וִידַעְתֶּם כִּי אֲנִי יְהוֹה אֱלֹהֵיכֶם
שֹׁכֵן בְּצִיּוֹן הַר קָדְשִׁי וְהָיְתָה יְרוּשָׁלִַם קֹדֶשׁ וְזָרִים
לֹא יַעַבְרוּ בָהּ עוֹד ׀ וְהָיָה בַיּוֹם הַהוּא יִטְּפוּ הֶהָרִים
עָסִיס וְהַגְּבָעוֹת תֵּלַכְנָה חָלָב וְכָל אֲפִיקֵי יְהוּדָה יֵלְכוּ
מָיִם וּמַעְיָן מִבֵּית יְהוֹה יֵצֵא וְהִשְׁקָה אֶת נַחַל הַשִּׁטִּים
מִצְרַיִם לִשְׁמָמָה תִהְיֶה וֶאֱדוֹם לְמִדְבַּר שְׁמָמָה
תִּהְיֶה מֵחֲמַס בְּנֵי יְהוּדָה אֲשֶׁר שָׁפְכוּ דָם נָקִיא
בְּאַרְצָם ׀ וִיהוּדָה לְעוֹלָם תֵּשֵׁב וִירוּשָׁלִַם לְדוֹר וָדוֹר
וְנִקֵּיתִי דָמָם לֹא נִקֵּיתִי וַיהוֹה שֹׁכֵן בְּצִיּוֹן

דברי

עָמוֹס אֲשֶׁר הָיָה בַנֹּקְדִים מִתְּקוֹעַ אֲשֶׁר חָזָה עַל
יִשְׂרָאֵל בִּימֵי עֻזִּיָּה מֶלֶךְ יְהוּדָה וּבִימֵי יָרָבְעָם בֶּן יוֹ
אָשׁ מֶלֶךְ יִשְׂרָאֵל שְׁנָתַיִם לִפְנֵי הָרָעַשׁ ׀ וַיֹּאמַר
יְהוֹה מִצִּיּוֹן יִשְׁאָג וּמִירוּשָׁלִַם יִתֵּן קוֹלוֹ וְאָבְלוּ נְאוֹת

29 (*Above*): Bible. Former and Latter
Prophets.
Opening of the Book of Amos. Germany; 14th
century. Copied by a scribe named
Meshullam.
[Add. MS 11637, f.321r.]

30 (*Right*): Pentateuch, with
prophetical readings and the Five
Scrolls.
Beginning of the Book of Numbers. Sefardi
(Spanish) hand. North Africa (?); 14th–15th
century.   [Add. MS 15283, f.114v.]

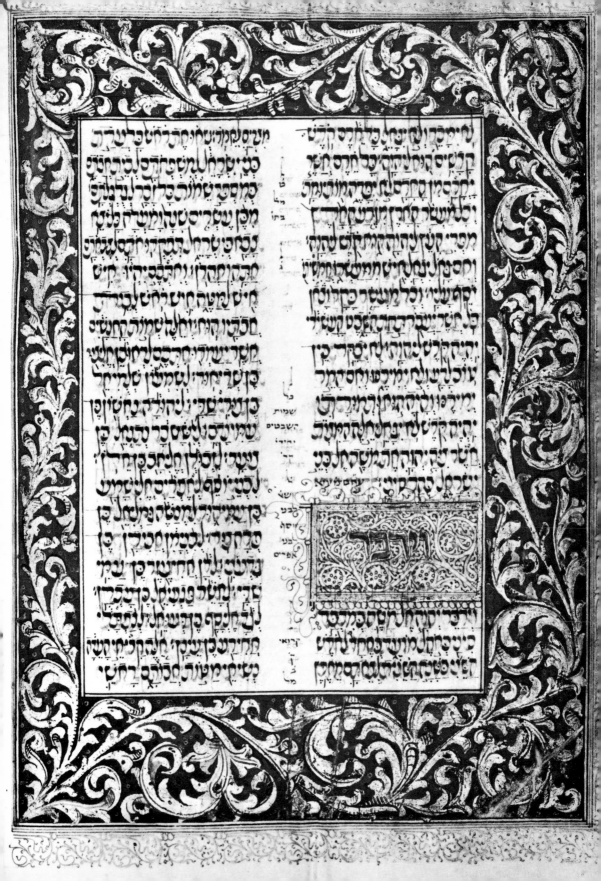

לבני ראובן ולגדים : מספר פקדת בני מנשה כי יוסף בני לפנים

ואחרי כן על פי משה ויעברו ... אלה המצות והמשפטים

אשר צוה יהוה ביד משה אל בני ישראל בערבות מואב על ירדן ירחו

אלה הדברים אשר דבר משה אל כל ישראל

בעבר הירדן במדבר בערבה מול סוף

בין פארן ובין תפל ולבן וחצרת ודי זהב

אחד עשר יום מחרב דרך הר שעיר עד

קדש ברנע : ויהי בארבעים שנה בעשתי

עשר חדש באחד לחדש דבר משה אל

בני ישראל ככל אשר צוה יהוה אתו אלהם : אחרי הכתו את סיחן

מלך האמרי אשר יושב בחשבון ואת עוג מלך הבשן אשר יושב

בעשתרות באדרעי : בעבר הירדן בארץ מואב הואיל משה באר

את התורה הזאת לאמר : יהוה אלהינו דבר אלינו בחרב לאמר

רב לכם שבת בהר הזה : פנו וסעו לכם ובאו הר האמרי ואל כל

שכניו בערבה בהר ובשפלה ובנגב ובחוף הים ארץ הכנעני

והלבנון עד הנהר הגדל נהר פרת : ראה נתתי לפניכם את הארץ

באו ורשו את הארץ אשר נשבע יהוה לאבתיכם לאברהם

ליצחק וליעקב לתת להם ולזרעם אחריהם : ואמר אלכם בעת

ההוא לאמר לא אוכל לבדי שאת אתכם : יהוה אלהיכם הרבה

אתכם והנכם היום ככוכבי השמים לרב : יהוה אלהי אבותכם יסף

עליכם ככם אלף פעמים ויברך אתכם כאשר דבר לכם : ואיכה

אשא לבדי טרחכם ומשאכם וריבכם : הבו לכם אנשים חכמים

ונבנים וידעים לשבטיכם ואשימם בראשיכם : ותענו אתי ותאמרו

31 (*Left*): Duke of
Sussex Italian
Pentateuch.
Beginning of Book of
Deuteronomy. Italy;
about 1400.
[Add. MS 15423. f.117r.]

32 (*Right*):
Fathnama.
(Book of the Conquest).
A poetical paraphrase in
Judeo–Persian by
Imrani of Shiraz of the
narratives in the Books
of Joshua, Ruth and
Samuel. Seven priests
circling Jericho, and
blowing rams' horns.
Persia; 17th century.
[Or. MS 13704, f.31v.]

hand artists can spend great energy on the Book of Psalms, every individual Psalm having its own decorated opening, as well as the Book itself. They also pick out for special attention the marginal letters which indicate the different weekly sections of the Torah.

The decoration of the Scroll of Esther was a comparatively late development in Jewish art, beginning in the 16th century. The story of Esther, which is picturesque in its own right, is illustrated frequently in panels above and below the text itself, the text space often being divided by architectural columns. The 17th century was the high-water mark of the genre, artists from Italy, France and the Netherlands being the most prominent.

Prayerbooks

After the Bible the prayerbook is the most honoured and cherished religious work in the Jewish home. The main structure of the liturgy both for communal and private worship was established more than 2,000 years ago, but it has been expanded considerably since then. There are also many differences of ritual practice between Sefardi and Ashkenazi communities, as well as a large number of local variations. The basic liturgy, however, remains uniform throughout.

There are three main types of prayerbook; the *Siddur*, the liturgy for weekdays and Sabbaths throughout the year; the *Machzor*, the prayer-book for the festivals; and the *Haggadah*, the order of service for the celebration of Passover-eve in the home.

The *Machzor* provides more scope for illustration than the *Siddur*, because most of the Jewish festivals are connected with historical episodes in the life of the Jewish people and with the seasons of the agricultural year. Thus a South German *Machzor* displays a harvest scene coupled with an illustration from the Book of Ruth (**51**), both being asssociated with the festival of *Shavuot* (Pentecost). This festival commemorates the revelation of the law at Mount Sinai, illustrated by a picture of Moses receiving the Ten Commandments (**52**).

Most of the decoration in these genres is concentrated on opening words not of the basic statutory prayers, but of the liturgical poems (*piyyutim*), which were composed in the middle ages, and quickly established themselves as integral elements of the synagogue service.

Of all Jewish prayer-books the *Haggadah* is the most extensively and richly decorated. *Haggadah* means literally 'narration'. It tells the story of the divine deliverance of the children of Israel from Egyptian bondage. On the eve of Passover the Jewish family, seated round a festive table, recreate, as it were, the experience of liberation from slavery. There are a number of symbolic foods on the table which together with specific rituals performed on the occasion prompt questions traditionally asked by the children. It is in answer to these questions that the head of the household tells the story of the Exodus. He thus fulfils the Biblical injunction: 'you shall tell your son . . . It is because of what the Lord did for me when I came out of Egypt'.

The *Haggadah* lends itself admirably to illustration. The story itself, with rabbinic elaboration, the meal, the different foods, the details of the ritual, all provide material on which the artist can exercise his skill. And the fact that the story is told to children is an additional incentive for colourful illustration.

There are certain pictorial elements which are common to practically all illuminated manuscript *Haggadot*: the meal (called *seder*, literally 'order', because the rituals are performed in a prescribed order), the *matsah* (unleavened bread), and the *maror* (bitter herbs). Other features frequently illustrated are: the four sons, whose questions reveal their different characters; drinking the statutory four cups of wine; the five rabbis of Bene Brak; the Hebrew slaves building cities for Pharaoh; the Exodus; and portraits of various rabbis mentioned in the text. In addition, the artist will usually decorate the opening words of each section. Spanish *Haggadot* sometimes have several full-page illustrations that precede the text proper. These illustrations narrate the story of the Exodus and the Passover ritual, beginning the Biblical account at a very early stage in the story. (The Sarajevo Haggadah, written in the 14th century, probably in Barcelona, actually begins its series of illustrations with the creation of the world.) This leaves the text itself with few accompanying illustrations. A superb example of this type is the British Library Golden Haggadah (46). The Barcelona Haggadah, however, follows a different method, and has illustrations throughout, practically every page being elaborately painted (33–38).

This practice of having the illustration side by side with the text that it depicts is followed also by the Ashkenazi *Haggadot*. Joel ben Simeon Feibusch, who lived in Bonn and Cologne in the 15th century, put his name to eleven extant illuminated Hebrew manuscripts, two of which, a *Haggadah* and a *Siddur*, are in the British Library collection. His *Haggadah* is remarkable for its large size (370 × 280 mm) and for its splendid calligraphy and illustrations, some of the latter being by other artists (see **45, 47, 48** and **front cover**).

The tradition of illustrating the *Haggadah* continued after the introduction of Hebrew printing at the end of the 15th century.

33, 34 Barcelona Haggadah.
Above: the Passover meal (*Seder*). The celebrant lifts a napkin
covering the *matsot* that are being carried fancifully on the head of
the boy next to him, and recites 'This is the bread of affliction'.
There are copies of *Haggadah* texts on the table. Note the lamps
above the table and the dogs below it. *Right*: The Passover meal,
showing the celebrant on the left breaking the *matsah*. The lady on
the right is shown concealing part of a *matsah*, in accordance with
the ritual. North Spain, probably Barcelona; mid-14th century.
[Add. MS 14761, ff. 28v, 20v.]

וַיִּקַּח

אֹתַת מִשְׁדֶשׁ הַמִּצְוֹת אֲ
אֲשֶׁר בְּסַל וּמֵזְגֵ אוֹתָה
לְשֻׁתֵּם וּמִנַּת חָזִיָּה כֵּן
שְׁתֵי הַשְּׁלֵמוֹת וְחָצֵהַם
חֲמִשָּׁה . וַיְחוּבֶּסֶר שְׁבֵי

35, 36 Barcelona Haggadah.
Above: the Hebrews building cities for Pharaoh, illustrating the scriptural verse 'they put upon us heavy work', the first Hebrew word of which is in the panel. *Right*: the Hebrews building cities for Pharaoh, illustrating the scriptural verse 'we were slaves to Pharaoh in Egypt'. An overseer mounted on a horse encourages a taskmaster to whip the slaves. At the foot of the page the Hebrews make bricks, which are then taken up by pulley. North Spain, probably Barcelona: mid-14th century.
[Add. MS 14761, ff.43r, 30v.]

ויקד העם וישתחוו

37, 38 Barcelona Haggadah.
Left: an elaborately decorated circular *matsah* (unleavened bread), containing eight shields, four of which resemble the arms of Barcelona. A bearded figure above holds two *matsot*. At the four corners 'putti' blow trumpets. In an arcade at the foot there are five musicians playing (from the left): pipe and tabor, viol, lute, bagpipes, nakers (kettle-drums). *Above*: interior of a synagogue. The reader on the left, clothed in a prayer shawl, holds a scroll of the Law (*Sefer Torah*) in its case. The text is Psalm 113, one of the *Hallel* Psalms. North Spain, probably Barcelona; mid-14th century.
[Add. MS 14761, f.65v.]

בעל הבית ובני ביתו יעשנים וקורר בליל פסח

39 (*Left*): Haggadah.
A decorated panel for the Passover song *Dayyenu* ('it would have sufficed'). Catalonia;
about 1360.   [Or. MS 1404, f.16r.]

40 (*Above*): Haggadah.
A family gathered at the table for the Passover meal (*Seder*). Two *haggadot* on the
table are open at the beginning of the *Seder* service: 'This is the bread of affliction'.
North Spain, Barcelona (?), about 1350.   [Or. MS 2884, f.18r.]

בעל הבית נגב ביינו שאומרים ההגדה

41 (*Above*): Haggadah.
A synagogue. The reader on a raised pulpit leads the
congregation below. North Spain, Barcelona (?),
about 1350.
[Or. MS 2884, f.17v.]

42 (*Right*): Haggadah.
Two illustrations of the Exodus: above, the Hebrews
leave Egypt; below, the Egyptians pursue them.
Catalonia; about 1460.
[Or. MS 1404, f.6v.]

וישא העם את בצקו טרם יחמץ משארתם צרות בשמלתם על שכמם ובני ישראל עשו כדבר משה

וישא את בצקו טרם יחמץ טרם יחפץ צרורת משארות בשמלותם על שכמם

וידחקו מצרים אחריהם וישינו אותם חונים על הים כל סוס רכב פרעה

וירדפו מצרים אחריהם וישיגו אותם חונים על הים כל סוס רכב פרעה ופרשיו וחילו על פי

פירוש אברבנאל

מַעְשֶׂה בְּרַבִּי אֱלִיעֶזֶר וְרַבִּי
יְהוֹשֻׁעַ וְרַבִּי א
אֶלְעָזָר בֶּן עֲזַרְיָה וְרַבִּי עֲקִיבָא וְרַבִּי
טַרְפוֹן שֶׁהָיוּ מְסוּבִּין בִּבְנֵי בְרַק וְהָיוּ
מְסַפְּרִים בִּיצִיאַת מִצְרַיִם כָּל אוֹתוֹ

50

43 (*Left*): Leipnik
Haggadah.
The five Rabbis of Bne Brak
who discussed the Passover all
night, until students arrived to
tell them that it was time for
morning prayers. Copied and
illuminated by Joseph Leipnik.
Altona; dated 1740.
[Sloane MS 3173, f.5v.]

44 South German
Machzor (Festival prayer-
book).
Prayers for *Shemini Atseret*
(Eighth Day of Assembly).
Initial word *om* (nation) of a
liturgical poem. Copied and
illuminated by Hayyim. South
Germany; about 1320.
[Add. MS 22413, f.131r. Detail.]

45 Feibusch Haggadah.
Decorated first word *Ometz*
(strength) of a Passover hymn.
Copied and illuminated by Joel
ben Simeon Feibusch and
others. South Germany; about
1460–1475.
[Add. MS 14762, f.45r.]

46 (*Left*): Golden
Haggadah.
Four biblical episodes. From
the top, right to left; the
Hebrew making bricks from
straw; the Hebrews building
cities for Pharaoh; Aaron's
rod swallowing the magicians'
rods; the plague of blood.
North Spain, Barcelona (?);
about 1320.
[Add. MS 27210, f.11r.]

47, 48 Feibusch
Haggadah.
Above: decorated first word
Hodu (Praise) of Psalm 136.
The green background
depicts a hunting scene.
Right: the wise son. He wears
the *arba kanfot*, the
traditional four-fringed
garment. Copied and
illuminated by Joel ben
Simeon Feibusch, and others.
South Germany; about
1460–1475.
[Add. MS 14762, ff.37v, 8v. Detail.]

49, 50 Forli Siddur (Prayers for the whole year).
Italian rite. *Left*: Rabban Gamaliel and his pupils, illustrating a passage in the *Haggadah*. *Right*: Scene in a synagogue. The figure on the right holds a *Sefer Torah*. Copied and illuminated by Moses Ziphroni for his father-in-law Daniel. Forli in the Romagna; dated 1383.
[Add. MS 26968, ff.118r.139v.]

51, 52 South German Machzor (Festival prayer-book).

Above: opening of the Book of Ruth, showing a harvest scene. Some of the figures have animal heads, an unexplained feature of manuscripts from this age and area. *Below*: Morning prayers for *Shavuot* (Pentecost); an illustration of Moses receiving the Ten Commandments, with Aaron and the elders of Israel behind him. Copied and illuminated by Hayyim. South Germany; about 1320.
[Add. MS 22413, ff.71r (detail), 3r.]

53 (*Opposite*): Machzor (Festival prayer-book). Roman rite. Decorated opening of the prayers for *Hanukkah* (Festival of Dedication). Italy; 15th century.
[Add. MS 16577, f.30v.]

עניין חנובה

מזמור

ער הנסים

Joseph Leipnik, the eighteenth-century scribe and artist from Germany, actually used a printed *Haggadah* as his source of inspiration (43). Some 3,000 editions of the *Haggadah* have been printed, many of them illustrated, frequently by Jewish artists of international renown.

Other manuscripts

Biblical and liturgical manuscripts are those most frequently illuminated, but they are not the only ones. Artists have embellished other types of literature, including works of philosophy, science, especially medicine, and codes of Jewish law. A magnificent example of the latter is the two volume manuscript of the *Mishneh Torah*, written by Moses ben Maimon (known as Maimonides) in Egypt in 1182, and copied in Lisbon nearly 300 years later by Solomon ibn Alzuk. The Introduction and each of the 14 books in which the work is arranged are elaborately decorated with foliage and flowers and delicate filigree work (55, 56).

The marriage contract (*Ketubah*) is another genre which attracted the skill of the artist. The joy and solemnity of the occasion are celebrated in many styles, varying from carpet designs in copies emanating from the Middle East and North Africa to the elaborate conceptions of the Italian Renaissance and the Baroque (54).

The introduction of printing profoundly affected the work of scribes and the artists who decorated their manuscripts. Naturally the magnificent but expensive Hebrew codices of Bible, liturgy and law gave way to the more easily accessible printed products. But the art of the Jewish scribe continued, because it was always essential (and still is) to the traditional Jewish religious life. Jewish law still requires that certain texts should be written by hand, ranging from scrolls of the Torah read in synagogues, to scriptural passages for *tefillin* (phylacteries) and *mezuzot* which are affixed to doorposts. The Jewish art of illumination also survived.

There was a strong revival of manuscript illumination of the liturgy, particularly *Haggadot*, in the 18th century in the Hamburg–Altona region of Germany (43) and also in Bohemia and Moravia. Decoration of the scroll of Esther continued. And there has been a marked reawakening of interest in the practice of the art in our own times, particularly in Israel and the United States.

55, 56 (*Overleaf*): Lisbon Mishneh Torah. A code of law by Moses Maimonides (1135–1204), the great lawyer, philosopher and physician. Opening of the Introduction. The fleshy leaves and delicate filigree work are typical of the Lisbon school. The manuscript is in two volumes. Copied by Solomon ibn Alzuk for Joseph ben David Ibn Yahya, Lisbon; dated A M 5232 (September 1471 – August 1472). [Harley MS 5698 (Vol. 1), ff.11v,12r.]

54 *Ketubah* (Marriage contract).
With margin in cut-out and backed by red paper. Illuminations include the twelve signs
of the zodiac, and illustrations of the biblical readings for the Sabbath following the
wedding date. The bridal pair were Ephraim Sanguini and Luna Faro. Written at
Modena, 1 October 1557.
[Or. MS 6706.]

אולאמוש בהבטאל
מצותיד

ביתדינו ודודקבל משמואל וביתדינו ואהיה
השילני מיוצאימיצריסהיהוליהישמעממשה
הורהשבכתב ומצוה זו פירושהתורהוהמיצוהתורה זו
רבנוהיהקטן במימשה והואקבל מדורוביתדינו
אליהוקבל מאהיה השילני וביתדינו ואלישעקבל
כלהתורהכתבנה משהשהרבט קודם שימותבכתבידו
ונתן ספרלכלשבטושבט וספראחד נתנהבארון
לעד שנאלקוה אתהספרהתורההוגני והמיצוה שהוא
פירוש התורהלא בתבהאלאצוהבה לזקנים
וליהושעולכל ישראלשנא את כלהדבר
אשראנכימצוה אתכם אותוהשמרולעשות וג
ומפניזה נקראת תורה שבעלפה ואעפ שלאנכתבה
תורה שבעלפה למדה משה רבנונכלה בביתדינו
לשבעים זקני ואלעזר ופנחס ויהושע שלשתם
קבלמימשה וליהושע שהוא תלמידושלמשה
רבנומסרלותורה שבעלפהוצוהו עליה וכן יהושע
למדכלימיו עלפה וזקנטרבים קבלומיהושע
וקבלעלים הזקנים ומפנחסושמואל קבלמעל

ביתדינו שנהנו לולמשה נכסיע בפירושן נתנו שנא
ואתנהלך אתלוחתהאבן והתורהוהמיצוהתורה זו
הורהשבכתב ומיצוה זו פירושוצונו לעשותהתורה
עלפיהמצוה ומיצוה זוהיא הנקראתתורה שבעלפה
כלהתורהכתבנה משהשהרבט קורם שימותבכתבידר
ונתן ספרלכלשבטושבט וספראחד נתנהבארון
לעד שנאלקוה אתהספרהתורההוגני והמיצוה שהוא
פירוש התורהלא בתבהאלאצוהבה לזקנים
וליהושעולכל ישראלשנא את כלהדבר
אשראנכימצוה אתכם אותוהשמרולעשות וג
ומפניזה נקראת תורה שבעלפה ואעפ שלאנכתבה
תורה שבעלפה למדה משה רבנונכלה בביתדינו
לשבעים זקני ואלעזר ופנחס ויהושע שלשתם
קבלמימשה וליהושע שהוא תלמידושלמשה
רבנומסרלותורה שבעלפהוצוהו עליה וכן יהושע
למדכלימיו עלפה וזקנטרבים קבלומיהושע
וקבלעלים הזקנים ומפנחסושמואל קבלמעל

פיסקי סדר ישועות

57, 58 Italian Code of Law.

Legal decisions of Isaiah ben Elijah di Trani, the Younger (died *c.* 1280). Copied by Jekuthiel ben Solomon for his teacher Menahem ben Nathan. *Left:* Beginning of *Baba Kamma*, on damages. The decoration is predominantly of red, blue and gold. The roundels alternate between animals and flower designs. The animals from the top are: bird, fox, ram's head, and bat. At the foot a hound bites a deer, possibly intended to illustrate an act for which damages must be paid. *Right:* Beginning of *Eruvin*, on the Sabbath limits. A man is shown marking out a boundary for the Sabbath. Italy, Dated 1374.
[Or. MS 5024, ff.171r, 40v.]

The British Library collections

The strength of the Hebrew manuscript collection in the British Library (there are more than 3,000 manuscripts in total) is due mainly to its judicious policy of acquisition which has continued almost without interruption since the foundation of the British Museum in 1753. In that year a collection of 130 Hebrew Manuscripts, the Harley collection, was purchased from the Countess of Oxford and Mortimer and the Duchess of Portland. Among these manuscripts was the beautiful Lisbon *Mishneh Torah* (**55, 56**). The Collection formed by Sir Hans Sloane, including the Leipnik Haggadah (**43**), was acquired in the same year. Among the books and manuscripts donated in 1823 by King George IV was one Hebrew manuscript, a Spanish Bible, recorded in the Catalogue as Kings MS, No. 1 (**21**).

In the 19th century the collection was enriched by the purchase in 1839 of the North French Miscellany (**13–18**) and five years later two magnificent *Haggadot* were bought from the dealers Payne and Foss, namely, the Barcelona *Haggadah* (figs **33–38**) and the Feibusch *Haggadah* (**45, 47, 48**). Almost at the same time Hebrew manuscripts from the Duke of Sussex collection were bought at auction. Many of these were magnificently illuminated and the Bibles among them are frequently exhibited in the Library (**4, 5, 6, 7, 8, 19, 20**).

In 1865 the largest collection of Hebrew manuscripts acquired up to that time was bought from Asher & Co. of Berlin. It consisted of 332 items that once belonged to the Library of Joseph Almanzi of Padua. The most renowned of the illuminated manuscripts in his Library was the Golden Haggadah (**1, 46**).

Purchases from other sources continued. The outstanding Lisbon Bible in three volumes (**25, 27**) was acquired from Benjamin Cohen of Bukhara in 1882. The most recent acquisitions of importance have come from the collection formed by David Solomon Sassoon. Among the illuminated manuscripts is the Judeo-Persian *Fathnama* (**32**) bought at auction in 1975.

Suggestions for further reading

J GUTMANN *Hebrew Manuscript Painting* London 1979

J LEVEEN *The Hebrew Bible in Art* London 1944

T AND M METZGER *Jewish Life in the Middle Ages. Illuminated Hebrew Manuscripts of the Thirteenth to the Sixteenth Centuries* New York 1983

B NARKISS *Hebrew Illuminated Manuscripts* Jerusalem 1969

64